THE
ARAB-ISRAELI
CONFLICT

IVAN MINNIS

RAINTREE
STECK-VAUGHN
RSVP PUBLISHERS

A Harcourt Company

Austin   New York
www.raintreesteckvaughn.com

First published 2003 by Raintree Steck-Vaughn Publishers, an imprint of Steck-Vaughn Company

Library of Congress Cataloging-in-Publication Data is available upon request.

Designed by AMR
Illustrated by Chartwell Illustrators
Originated by Dot Gradations
Printed by South China Printers

ISBN 0-7398-6340-1

Printed in Hong Kong.

1 2 3 4 5 6 7 8 9 0 LB 06 05 04 03 02

Acknowledgments
The publishers would like to thank the following for permission to reproduce photographs:
pg. 5 Rex Features/S Frischling; pg. 7 Rex Features; pg. 9 Popperfoto; pg. 11 [top] Spaarnestad Fotoarchief [bottom] Hulton Getty/Hans Haim Pinn Photoservice; pg. 13 Popperfoto; pg. 15 Rex Features; pg. 17 Hulton Getty; pg. 18 Popperfoto; pg. 19 Popperfoto; pg. 20 Popperfoto; pg. 22 Associated Press; pg. 25 Hulton Getty; pg. 26 Hulton Getty; pg. 28 Hulton Getty; pg. 30 Hulton Getty; pg. 31 Popperfoto; pg. 33 Hulton Getty; pg. 35 Rex Features/Sipa Press; pg. 36 Popperfoto; pg. 37 Rex Features; pg. 38 Popperfoto; pg. 41 Hulton Getty; pg. 42 Popperfoto/Reuters; pg. 44 Rex Features/Sipa Press; pg. 46 Rex Features; pg. 47 Los Angeles Times; pg. 48 Popperfoto; pg. 51 Rex Features/Villard; pg. 52 Rex Features/Reardon; pg. 54 Popperfoto; pg. 55 Popperfoto; pg. 57 Press Association; pg. 58 European Press Agency.

Cover photograph reproduced with permission of Panos Pictures.

Every effort has been made to contact copyright holders of any material reproduced in this book. Any omissions will be rectified in subsequent printings if notice is given to the publishers.

Contents

The Struggle in the Middle East 4

The Holy Land 1: The Jews 8

The Holy Land 2: The Arabs 12

Turning Point: The British Mandate and the Creation of Israel..16

The Suez-Sinai War of 1956 20

The Six-Day War of 1967..24

Turning Point: Yom Kippur War of 1973 28

Turning Point: Camp David 32

Turning Point: War in Lebanon 36

A Global Conflict 40

The Media and the Conflict 44

Turning Point: Hopes for Peace 48

A False Dawn? 52

The Future 58

Timeline 60

Glossary 62

Index 64

Words that first appear in the text in bold, **like this,** are explained in the Glossary.

The Struggle in the Middle East

The Middle East is an area extending from the Persian Gulf to the eastern end of the Mediterranean. For centuries **nomadic** tribes roamed its deserts and plains in search of grazing for their livestock, occasionally settling around an oasis or river to build the ancient towns and cities that still stand today. Three continents, Europe, Asia, and Africa, meet in the Middle East, which helped the region to become a center for trade and learning in ancient times. Its rivers and seas formed trade routes bringing exotic spices and incense from the Far East and Africa to Western Europe and beyond. Trading encouraged the spread of new ideas and the area became the home of three of the world's major religions: Christianity, **Islam,** and **Judaism**. The importance each faith places on the area has led to conflict for centuries.

During the 19th century the construction of the Suez Canal, connecting the Mediterranean and Red Seas, increased the region's importance as a trade route, providing new and faster routes from Europe to India and the Pacific. However, the discovery of vast quantities of oil in the area during the 20th century made the Middle East more significant than ever. Without oil from the region, the **developed world** would grind to a halt. World leaders, therefore, watch closely each new development in the region.

The Emergence of Israel

The 20th century saw the breakup of the once great **Ottoman Empire**, with many **Arab** nations gaining their independence. In 1948 the new state of Israel was created, and many **Jews** returned to their ancient homeland. Their arrival in the region angered many Arabs, who regarded their Jewish neighbors as a threat to Arab unity. The creation of Israel brought war, with Arab nations determined to crush the new state before it could take root. Israel was able to survive but thousands of **Palestinians** were forced to live in refugee camps in neighboring states. Over the next fifty years war and violence became common; the existence of the state of Israel was a constant point of conflict in the region. Inevitably the international community has found itself being drawn into this conflict, often with terrible consequences.

American Jews protest against the peace negotiations between Shimon Peres and Yasser Arafat.

Superpower Rivalry

Israel emerged as an independent state at the end of the 1940s, a time when the World War II alliance of the United States and the Soviet Union was beginning to disintegrate. The tense relationship between these two great **superpowers** led to the **Cold War**. Both sides wanted to increase their power but the threat of nuclear weapons made direct conflict between them impossible. Instead both powers tried to extend their influence over other nations by providing them with weapons and financial aid. In doing so they hoped to befriend governments and gain their support in times of crisis.

The new countries of the Middle East soon found themselves at the center of this superpower rivalry. The United States has been very supportive of Israel, with America's large Jewish population lobbying for support of the new state. The United States also tried to maintain friendly governments in some Arab states, such as Saudi Arabia. Meanwhile the Soviet Union extended its influence among other Arab countries, such as Syria and Egypt, providing them with weapons and aid in their attempt to defeat Israel.

Trade

The construction of the Suez Canal during the mid-19th century opened up the Red Sea and Indian Ocean to European ships sailing out of the Mediterranean. The canal was of particular importance to the British, who regarded it as a vital route to parts of their Empire such as India and Australia. A desire to keep control of this canal, and to maintain a friendly government in Egypt, was central to Britain's involvement in the early years of the Arab-Israeli struggle.

Oil

The discovery of vast quantities of oil in the region increased the importance of the Middle East. Arab states, aware of the power their oil gives them, have limited production during times of crisis, forcing western powers to intervene and put pressure on Israel. Arab use of this "oil weapon" (for instance, see pages 30–31) has ensured that developed nations cannot afford to ignore instability and conflict in the area.

American Involvement in the Middle East

As you will see later in the book, the United States, the Soviet Union, and the **United Nations (UN)** have intervened in several of the wars and crises that have developed between the Arab states and the Israelis. Many Arab states have resented this interference, especially that of the United States. As a result some are willing to give support to Islamic groups that use terrorism and the taking of hostages to call attention to their stand against Israel. For many of these groups, U.S. support for Israel makes American **citizens**, both military and **civilian**, targets for terrorist attack.

The United States has shown itself willing to intervene to protect its interests in the region. In 1986 President Reagan launched air strikes against Libya, whose government he accused of supporting Islamic terrorists who were targeting American citizens.

"Israel stepped up its military offensive today, leaving about 30 Palestinians dead in raids on refugee camps and the town of Ramallah, the West Bank headquarters of Yasir Arafat. In a separate incident at least seven Israelis died in an attack near the border with Lebanon."
From the New York Times, *March 12, 2002*

The International Community

The Arab-Israeli conflict has raged for over fifty years despite the intervention of many western governments and the UN. UN peacekeepers have been based on the Sinai Peninsula and in Beirut in an attempt to prevent the conflict from escalating. Meanwhile the UN has been at the center of diplomatic moves to try to find a resolution to the conflict. The United States has also pushed hard for a solution, often pressing its Israeli allies into negotiations.

Jerusalem: The Holy City

During the reign of King Solomon, around 1000 B.C., a great building program was undertaken in Jerusalem. The most significant building erected was the Great Temple, the center of Judaism. The temple was destroyed by the Romans during the first Jewish revolt of A.D. 70 and eventually built over, leaving only the "Wailing Wall," the holiest site for modern Jews.

The city also has great significance for **Muslims**. They believe that at the end of the prophet Mohammed's life he was miraculously taken from Mecca to Jerusalem. From there he ascended in seven stages into heaven. Both Muslims and Jews, therefore, regard Jerusalem as central to their faith, and control of the city is of great importance to them.

The Old City of Jerusalem. The Dome of the Rock, one of Islam's most holy sites, can be seen rising above the Walled City.

The Holy Land 1: The Jews

The state of Israel is one of the world's newest countries, but the land has a long and troubled history. Both Jews and Arabs claim to be the rightful owners of the land, and each states that its religion and history justify its presence.

The Jews

The Old Testament tells the story of how Abraham made an agreement with God, which promised Abraham and his descendants the ancient land of Canaan (partly present-day Palestine). The "promised land" was colonized by Abraham's descendants. His son Jacob was also known as Israel, providing the name for the new "Israelites."

The Bible also tells how the Israelites were forced by famine to leave their land in around 2000 B.C. and settle in Egypt. The pharaohs enslaved them until Moses led them home around 1300 B.C. A further time of **exile** followed in the 6th century B.C., this time in Babylonia (roughly modern Iraq and Syria), but again the Israelites were able to return to their homeland, now known as Palestine.

During the first century B.C. Palestine was invaded by the Romans. The Jews could not accept the many Roman gods or the culture of the Empire. Their rebellions were put down with great violence that saw the destruction of Jerusalem and its Great Temple. Again the Jews were exiled and scattered across Europe—a condition known as the **Diaspora**—where they would be less troublesome to their rulers. They would not return for almost 2,000 years.

The Jews in Exile

Following their exile by the Romans, the Jews were unable to find a welcoming home anywhere in Europe. Christians regarded them with suspicion and hatred. These were the people, they said, who had called for Christ's crucifixion. The Jews maintained their customs and religion, making them different from their neighbors. They were viewed as strange and provided easy scapegoats in times of crisis. Jews were blamed for the plague, the disappearance of children, and political plots. Thus, from time to time throughout the following centuries, they met with persecution. They were expelled from England in 1292 and from Spain in 1492, and were greatly persecuted during the 1880s in Russia. A series of bloody attacks across Russia, known as **pogroms**, left thousands of Jews dead.

Theodor Herzl, the father of modern Zionism.

Zionism

The Russian pogroms left many Jews believing that they could live in peace only if they were able to return to their "homeland." This belief became known as **Zionism**, from the old Jewish name for Palestine, Zion.

Jews began to drift back to Palestine in 1882, setting up a colony near the city of Jaffa. Money from rich supporters enabled more to follow. Their leader was Theodor Herzl, a Hungarian Jew who wanted a separate Jewish state to allow his people to escape **anti-Semitism** in Europe. This state, he suggested, could be in Palestine or Argentina. At the first Zionist Congress, in 1897, it was agreed that Palestine was the better option and a fund was set up to buy land for Jewish settlers.

The events of World War II (1939–1945) proved still further the need for a homeland. The persecution of centuries reached its climax with the **Holocaust**. The Nazis, feeding off widespread European anti-Semitism, murdered over six million Jews in extermination camps such as Auschwitz. Those Jews who survived had lost everything: homes, families, businesses, and, perhaps most important, their trust in their European neighbors. They were more determined than ever to start new lives in Palestine.

The Holocaust also stirred the leaders of the West into action. Evidence of the Holocaust filtering into the media aroused public sympathy for the Jews. This was especially true in the United States, which had a large and powerful Jewish community. Jewish immigration to Palestine rocketed and Great Britain, which ruled the area as a mandate, was powerless to prevent the country from sliding into a conflict that has continued for almost 50 years.

A Siege Society

Early Jewish victories were no guarantee of the survival of their young country. Israel is surrounded by its Arab neighbors, military powers that are openly hostile to the Israelis. As a result, Israel is a nation that regards itself as being under constant threat of attack. The memories of the Holocaust are fresh and Israel is determined to take measures to defend itself, regardless of the opinions of either the Middle East or the rest of the world. They have therefore been prepared to seize land in other countries—Egypt, Jordan, and Lebanon—in order to create **buffer** zones to lessen the impact of any Arab attack. To Jews, Jerusalem has become a symbol of independence and determination to survive in the face of widespread opposition and hostility.

An Orthodox or a Secular Society

The early Zionists believed the word "Jewish" described a national identity. In 1948, the then Prime Minister David Ben-Gurion signed the "religious status quo" agreement. It required that the Sabbath (Saturday) and Kashrut (Jewish dietary law) be officially observed in the state. Civil marriages were not allowed and the Ultra-**Orthodox** were provided with an independent educational system. This was designed to appease the Orthodox Jews who maintain strict observance of religious laws.

However, since then, Israel's population has grown and changed. While Orthodox Jews make up 20 to 30 percent of the population, **secular** Jews and ethnically Russian and Ethiopian Jews find the laws a burden on their daily life. This divide has important implications for the peace process. Orthodox Jews and their sympathizers in the **Knesset** (the Israeli Parliament) are strongly opposed to negotiations with the Palestinians and form a powerful lobby in the country.

Prisoners being liberated from Dachau concentration camp at the end of World War II.

"Next Year in Jerusalem"

A return to their ancient homeland in Palestine has always been at the heart of the Jewish faith. For centuries Jews throughout the world consoled themselves at **Passover** festivals with the prayer, "Next year in Jerusalem." The terrible events of the Holocaust made the Jews even more determined to have their own state, and to defend it once achieved. One Israeli broadcaster summed up this strength of feeling: "I don't believe in the Jews' historical right to take land from other people because we were here 2,000 years ago. We have the right because of the Holocaust."

The ship *Jewish State* arriving in Haifa with 2,000 Jewish refugees from Nazi Germany on board. World sympathy for the Jews was aroused when the British, who feared Arab violence, turned it away.

The Holy Land 2: The Arabs

The 7th century A.D. saw the development of a new religion in the Middle East: Islam. The prophet Mohammed, born in Mecca in A.D. 570, brought this new religion to the Arab people. To the Arabs, Mohammed was the greatest of all prophets and after his death their armies began to spread his ideas throughout the Middle East and North Africa. For 500 years the Arabs ruled a great empire, extending from Spain to India and including Palestine, but after centuries of decline, they eventually came under Turkish rule in the 16th century. Unlike the Jews, however, the Arabs remained in Palestine.

Arab Nationalism

By 1914 the Arab people had been ruled by the Turks for four hundred years. They felt that their culture and economic development had been held back by the Turks, leaving them poor and backward. So, when Turkey sided with Germany in World War I, the Arabs were willing and eager to join with Great Britain in an attempt to free their country.

In return for Arab support, Great Britain promised to help set up an Arab state in the Middle East, which the Arabs assumed would include Palestine. The end of the war did not bring Arab independence, however. Instead, the **League of Nations** put the region in the hands of European powers. British control of Palestine saw the start of large-scale Jewish immigration into the country, with an often violent response from the Arab community. After one particularly violent attack on Jewish settlers in 1929, the British inquiry concluded that "the Palestinians have come to see [the Jews] not only as a menace to their livelihood but a possible overlord of the future." The report turned out to be prophetic.

A People Without a Homeland

In 1948, there were approximately 860,000 Palestinians in what is today's Israel. About 700,000 were driven out or fled during the fighting that followed the declaration of Israeli statehood in 1948. The Palestinian population of Jerusalem went from 75,000 to 3,500; of Jaffa from 70,000 to 3,600; of Haifa from 71,000 to 2,900. The refugees were dispersed into camps in neighboring Arab states. The 160,000 Palestinians still in Israel in 1949 lost much of their land, leaving them with no resources or strong leaders.

Refugees at Ramallah in 1948. Thousands of Palestinians fled their homes, their families forced to remain in camps for the next 50 years.

Although defeated in the 1948 war (see pages 18–19), the Palestinians refused to accept the new state of Israel. Like the Jews of the Diaspora, they now dream of a return to their homeland. In his address to the United Nations in 1974 Yasir Arafat, the Palestinian leader, made clear the Palestinian position: "It [the conflict] is the cause of a people deprived of its homeland, dispersed and uprooted, living mostly in **exile** and in refugee camps." The anthem of the **Palestinian Liberation Organization (PLO)** goes further: "Palestine is our country. Our aim is to return. Death does not frighten us, Palestine is ours."

Other Arab Organizations

Aside from the PLO, other Palestinian and Islamic **guerrilla** groups have influenced the conflict:

- The Popular Front for the Liberation of Palestine (PFLP) and the Black September Organization both emerged in the early 1970s, carrying out terrorist attacks such as the kidnapping of Israeli athletes at the Munich Olympics in 1972.
- The 1982 Israeli invasion of Lebanon saw the appearance of Islamic **militia** groups such as Hezbollah and Amal, which have targeted Israel and the United States.
- During the 1987 **Intifada** (Arabic for "uprising"), a new Palestinian group, HAMAS, was formed by Palestinians unhappy with the more moderate approach adopted by the PLO. Today, it has substantial support in the **Occupied Territories**, and is viewed as a threat to the peace process.

13

The Palestinian Liberation Organization

In 1964, the Arab states and various Palestinian groups formed the Palestine Liberation Organization (PLO). Although it has been accused of being a political tool of various Arab states, in 1974 the Arab countries recognized the PLO as the "sole legitimate representative of the Palestinian people." By that time, the PLO was headed by Yasir Arafat, the founder of Fatah, a political and military group that had become the PLO's most important constituent organization.

Under Arafat's leadership the PLO has adopted a variety of tactics throughout the conflict. Regarded by some as freedom fighters and by others as terrorists, it has fought pitched battles with the Israelis, as well as using bombing campaigns, hijacking, and assassination to further its cause.

Since the late 1980s the PLO has moved toward more moderate policies. Rather than aiming to destroy Israel, it has entered into talks aimed at achieving a negotiated settlement. It is now effectively regarded by all in the talks as the voice of the Palestinian people. After the Oslo Peace Accords in 1993, the PLO assumed control of parts of the **Occupied Territories**.

In the years since the Oslo Accords, the PLO's influence has been challenged by the Islamic fundamentalist group HAMAS. (In Arabic, the name is an acronym for Islamic Resistence Movement.) Particularly among young Palestinians, HAMAS is seen as being more militant than the PLO, whch is regarded by some as being corrupt and too willing to compromise with Israel.

Profile: Yasir Arafat (1929–)

While studying for an engineering degree in Cairo during the 1960s Yasir Arafat helped found Fatah, a Palestinian guerrilla group. Soon afterward, Fatah became part of the PLO, effectively its military wing. Arafat was made overall leader of the PLO in 1969. In 1974 he addressed the **UN** General Assembly, famously with a pistol strapped to his waist. He promised further violence unless a Palestinian state was created.

The campaign did continue, but Arafat's position as leader was far from secure when the 1982 Israeli invasion of Lebanon forced him from his Beirut base. However, he remained in control and, from 1988 onward, led the PLO toward negotiations with Israel. Arafat fell out of favor with the international community for his support of Iraq during the Gulf War (see page 50), but the successful negotiations that led to the Oslo Peace Accords restored his credibility. In 1994, a year after formally signing the Accords in Washington, Arafat was awarded the Nobel Peace Prize along with the Israeli Prime Minister Yitzhak Rabin and his foreign minister Shimon Peres.

With self-rule returning to parts of the West Bank and Gaza, Arafat was elected president of the newly created Palestinian Authority in 1996, with a huge majority.

Yasir Arafat, President of the Palestinian Authority.

Turning Point: The British Mandate and the Creation of Israel

The Balfour Declaration
In November 1917 the British foreign secretary, Arthur Balfour, wrote to leading **Zionists** declaring that Great Britain would support their plans for a homeland in Palestine. Arabs were furious, knowing that if this were the case it would be at the expense of their people in Palestine. Great Britain assured them that plans for a united Arab state were unaffected, but the British government nevertheless continued to favor the Zionist demands.

The Treaty of Versailles
Great Britain's attitude became of greater importance after World War I. The Treaty of Versailles gave control of much of Turkey's Middle Eastern empire to the British. The peacemakers wanted the peoples of the defeated empire to be able to rule themselves, but felt that they were not yet ready. Britain ruled the area as a "**mandate**," preparing the people for self-government. To Jews the **British Mandate** appeared to be an opportunity to put their plans into action.

The British Mandate
The years of British rule in Palestine saw increasing violence, as Arabs reacted angrily to the arrival of Jewish settlers, with immigration figures set at 16,500. Arab riots in 1921 led to a reduction in the number of Jews allowed into Palestine, but the number of Zionist settlements continued to grow. In 1929 extreme Zionists demonstrated near the Dome of the Rock in Jerusalem, leading to mass rioting by Arabs in which over 100 Jews were killed.

With Hitler's rise to power in Germany, even more Jews fled Europe and immigration rose to 61,000 in 1935. The Arab leaders called a general strike in an attempt to force a change in British policy. They were successful, but the change was not what they desired. The British announced that Palestine would be divided into an Arab and a Jewish state, with half of the country allocated to the Zionists. The Arabs immediately rebelled, but by 1939 had been defeated by stronger British forces. The outbreak of World War II in September 1939 temporarily united most Jews and Arabs behind the British, but the problem had not been resolved. The terrible events of the Holocaust were about to transform both Europe and the Middle East.

The Arabs continued to resist British rule even after their decisive defeat in 1939.

On July 22, 1946, a bomb exploded in the King David Hotel, headquarters of the British military in Palestine. Members of "Irgun," a Jewish terrorist group, disguised as Arabs, were responsible for the bombing. The resulting explosion killed 88 people, including 15 Jews. The bomb clearly demonstrated the lengths to which Zionists would go to expel the British from Palestine in their efforts to create a homeland for the Jews.

The violence continued as the British attempted to limit the number of Jews gaining entry to Palestine—Jewish refugees fleeing Europe after the horrors of the Holocaust. Eventually, in February 1947, the British announced plans to withdraw, unable to sustain troop levels of 100,000 in the **austere** postwar years. Instead it was proposed that Palestine be handed over to the control of the United Nations.

Partition

The UN decided that the only possible solution was to divide Palestine into separate Jewish and Arab states. Although they made up only one third of the population, the Jews were to be given a greater share of the land in anticipation of more immigration. Inevitably the Arabs rejected the plan, not wanting to give up so much of their land. The Jews and the Holocaust, it was argued, were the responsibility of Europe, not of the Arabs. Palestinian Jews were also unhappy about the proposed boundaries, since they left Jerusalem in the heart of the Arab zone. The holy city of three religions would come under the control of the UN, but control of the access roads was in Arab hands.

A member of the Haganah on sentry duty during the 1948 war.

War of Independence

In the buildup to British withdrawal, violence between the Jews and Arabs increased as both sides tried to gain control of the roads leading to Jerusalem. Soldiers from Syria and Iraq prepared to come to the aid of their Arab neighbors, while the Jewish **Haganah** organized the defense of Jewish areas. More extreme elements within the Jewish community began to attack Arab settlements. By the time the British withdrew in May 1948, more than 300,000 Arabs had fled Jewish areas.

War of Independence

"Tens of thousands of our youth are prepared to lay down their lives for the sake of Jerusalem. It is within the boundaries of the state of Israel, just as Tel Aviv is."
David Ben-Gurion, first prime minister of Israel

Year of Catastrophe

"The Palestinian problem is the story of a people who lived peacefully in their own homes for generations. Then along came total strangers who turned the people out of their country and occupied their homes."
S. Hadawi, an Arab writer

Despite initial confidence and optimism, the Arab forces were disorganized and had difficulty defending the long borders of the Arab zone. The Haganah, operating from the much smaller area they controlled, was able first to resist the Arab onslaught and then to drive them back, capturing large parts of what the UN had declared to be Arab territory. By January of 1949 the two sides came to an uneasy truce, and the state of Israel had survived its first assault.

Year of Catastrophe

While to the Jews 1948 was a year of independence, to the Arabs it became their "year of catastrophe." Thousands died in the fighting, some in full-scale massacres. In April 1948 about 80 members of the Irgun, led by the future prime minister of Israel, Menachem Begin, attacked the Arab village of Deir Yassin. They killed the entire population of the village, leading to widespread panic among the Arab population. About 700,000 Arabs fled their homes, as further areas of Palestine came under Jewish control. Defeated in the civil war, the Palestinians were now a people without a homeland. They were forced to seek sanctuary in neighboring Arab states. However, their former allies found it difficult to absorb these refugees, who were not assimilated into the local population. Instead the Palestinians lived in huge refugee camps close to the Israeli border, waiting for an opportunity to regain their lands.

Profile: David Ben-Gurion 1886–1973

Ben-Gurion was born in Poland but emigrated to Palestine in 1906. He helped organize the Haganah, the secret Jewish defense force of the 1930s and 1940s. He came to prominence as a Zionist spokesman between 1942 and 1948. When the British withdrew, he proclaimed Israel a new state. He was prime minister from 1948 to 1953, and from 1955 to 1963, and is regarded as the architect of modern Israel.

David Ben-Gurion, proclaiming the birth of the new Jewish state, May 24, 1948.

The Suez-Sinai War of 1956

After its victory in the "War of Independence," the new state of Israel was weak and surrounded by enemies. The homeland dreamed of by the Zionists opened its doors to Jews from all over Europe and the Middle East. By the end of 1951, 657,000 Jews had swelled the population—immigrants as committed to Zionism as their predecessors. Slowly, supported by the wealth of the United States, the fledgling state was able to grow in confidence.

The Arab Reaction

The Arab world had been stunned by its defeat in the war. Old regimes were replaced with more **nationalistic** young leaders who wanted to modernize their countries. These leaders turned against the West, particularly the United States and Great Britain, regarding them as interfering Zionists. They aimed instead to create a united Arab world able to act as one in areas of common interest.

The Palestinians, meanwhile, found themselves a people without a state. Their Arab neighbors refused to grant them citizenship, condemning them to a future in refugee camps. Some were prepared to fight to regain their lands. The **Fedayeen** (Arabic for "self-sacrificers") launched attacks against the Israelis almost as soon as the War of 1948 ended. The Israelis hit back, attacking not only the Fedayeen but also their Arab neighbors. With each passing year, the Fedayeen attacks and Israeli **reprisals** further heightened tensions in the Middle East.

With its twin city of Jaffa, Tel Aviv is Israel's cosmopolitan, secular center.

Nasser and Arab Nationalism

In Egypt in 1952, young army officers overthrew the corrupt pro-British regime of King Farouk. Two years later Colonel Nasser took control, forcing a British withdrawal from positions around the Suez Canal, a vital trade route for oil from the region. Nasser immediately began an extensive program of modernization. Factories, hospitals, and schools were built, and plans were proposed for a huge dam at Aswan to provide more agricultural land.

Relationships between Egypt and the western powers became increasingly strained under Nasser. In 1955, under pressure from those in his government who wanted a stronger military, he turned to the Soviet Union for arms supplies. Great Britain and the United States feared that the Soviet Union was attempting to gain influence in the Middle East. They showed their anger by canceling loans offered to support Nasser's most prestigious project, the Aswan Dam.

The Suez Canal

The Suez Canal is an important trade route, linking the Mediterranean Sea to the Indian Ocean. Without it, ships sailing from Europe to the Far East would be forced to sail around the south of Africa, adding thousands of miles to their journeys. Until 1956 Great Britain and France owned the canal.

When the loans for the Aswan dam were canceled, Nasser reacted swiftly, announcing that he would nationalize the canal. Instead of the profits going to Great Britain and France, Egypt would use the money to help pay for the country's modernization. This was the last straw for the British and French. They regarded the canal as vital to their navies and trade, and feared that Nasser might close it to them, or use it as a bargaining tool. The two governments decided that Nasser had to be overthrown, but they could not risk angering other Arab states.

Knowing that they could not invade Egypt themselves, the British and French governments entered into secret negotiations with Israel. A plan emerged for Israel to attack Egypt, destroying the Fedayeen in Sinai and advancing to the Suez Canal. Britain and France would then demand that both sides withdraw from the canal zone. If, as they expected, Nasser refused to withdraw they would send in troops, claiming that they were there to stop the fighting and keep the canal open. The plan had risks. Great Britain and France insisted on keeping the plan a secret from the

United States, which had warned them not to use force in the region. The Israelis feared that secrecy would anger the Americans, who had supported them since 1945. However, their prime minister, David Ben-Gurion, thought it important to strike against Egypt and was willing to accept French weapons that would allow him to do so.

The Fighting Begins

On October 29, 1956, Israel sent its troops into the Sinai Peninsula. Egyptian communications had been cut and Israeli forces were able to make great gains in the area. As planned, Great Britain and France demanded that both sides withdraw 10 miles (16 km) from the

Colonel Gamal Abdel Nasser.

Suez Canal. When Nasser refused, air strikes were launched against Egypt's airfields, destroying many planes on the ground. Free from air attacks, the Israeli forces were able to occupy most of the Sinai, before British and French paratroopers landed to the north at Port Said.

Profile: Colonel Gamal Abdel Nasser (1918–1970)

The son of a post office worker, Nasser became an officer in the Egyptian Army in 1938. He was angered by Egypt's failure to defeat Israel in 1948 and masterminded the 1952 plot that overthrew King Farouk. As president he introduced reforms that improved life for ordinary Egyptians but he was unable to create the United Arab Republic he hoped for, since his military dependence on the Soviet Union worried many Arab leaders. Egypt's crushing defeat by Israel in 1967 reduced his influence in the Arab world, but he remained popular at home until his death in 1970.

The Aftermath
Although the military campaign appeared to be going well for Great Britain, France, and Israel, there was an international outcry over their actions. In Great Britain, public opinion was against the attack and the government itself came under attack from all sides. The United States government was furious and, through the United Nations Security Council, demanded an immediate **ceasefire**. The British and French **vetoed** the proposal.

With the western powers in disarray, the Soviet Union made it clear that it was prepared to send troops into the area to assist Egypt. The United States could not risk such a move, and threatened to withdraw oil supplies to Great Britain and France. With supplies from Arab states drying up, the two governments were forced into an embarrassing withdrawal. United Nations peacekeepers took over their positions along the canal.

Results of the War
The Suez-Sinai war was a disaster for Great Britain and France. Great Britain's decline as a world power was clear, as was its reliance on the United States. Great Britain's role and influence in the Middle East were greatly reduced as Arab states turned instead to the Soviet Union for backing. Pro-British Arab states, such as Iraq and Lebanon, turned against them, leaving the United States to try to check Soviet influence.

For Israel the war was a military success. They had defeated the Egyptians and crushed the Fedayeen. In January 1957 they were forced by the UN to withdraw from the Sinai Peninsula, but despite losing their territorial gains, they had still improved their position. A UN peacekeeping force patrolled the Sinai border, preventing further Arab attacks in the area and reopening the Gulf of Aqaba to Israeli shipping.

Although defeated in the war, Nasser's reputation as leader of the Arab world grew. He was respected for standing up to the western powers and winning a diplomatic victory. With Nasser at its head, it appeared possible that the Arab world would soon fall under the influence of the Soviet Union.

The Six-Day War of 1967

Between 1956 and 1967 an uneasy peace prevailed in the Middle East. In Israel there were signs that the country was struggling to cope with its independence. The economy was in difficulty, and unemployment was high. There were many strikes and demands for higher wages. It was an uncertain time politically, since there was not an obvious successor to Ben-Gurion. However, to the outside world Israel seemed to be a unified, progressive nation.

Changes in the Arab World

The Arabs also had their troubles. After the Suez-Sinai War in 1956, Nasser emerged as the most prominent figure in the Arab world. With the Soviet Union's help he had attempted to rebuild Egypt's military power and was largely responsible for the coming together of Egypt and Syria and the formation of the United Arab Republic (UAR).

Egypt and Syria hoped that shared interests would allow them to unite under a single government, but splits soon emerged. Many groups in Syria, especially the military, felt that the UAR parliament was dominated by Egyptians. The UAR collapsed after two years, shattering Nasser's dream of Arab unity, but the two nations continued to be united by one important thing—a hatred of the Israelis.

Elsewhere in the Arab world there was political turmoil. A new political group, the Baath party, had emerged to threaten established governments. Its policies were a mixture of **communism** and Arab nationalism, centered on anti-Israeli feelings. In Iraq the Baath party took over from the military dictator General Abdul Karim Kassem in 1963 but was soon replaced by another military dictatorship under General Abd as-Salam Aref. Syria was also experiencing a hard fight for control among left-wing groups, resulting in a victory for the Baath party, which seized power in 1966.

Tension Mounts

In 1964 the Palestinian Liberation Organization (PLO) was formed, replacing the Fedayeen. It began a bombing campaign in Israel. Buildings close to the Knesset, the Israeli parliament house, were destroyed and bombs exploded among crowds at soccer matches. The PLO attacks came mainly from bases in Syria, now allied with Egypt, and Israel countered with attacks deep into Syrian territory. Syrian guns maintained a constant rain of attacks on northern Israel, shelling Israeli settlements from the Golan Heights. In April 1967 the Israelis retaliated, bombing the Syrian guns before flying on to the capital of Damascus in a clear show of strength.

Prelude to War

The tension was increased by Russian intelligence warnings that Israel intended to launch a full-scale attack against Syria. Nasser came under pressure to show leadership, condemned by both Syria and Jordan for his lack of action. On May 16, he made his intentions clear, ordering the withdrawal of UNEF (United Nations Emergency Force) from the Sinai Peninsula. This UN force had patrolled the area since the 1956 war, acting as a buffer between Egypt and Israel. Their departure was marked by the arrival of the Egyptian army. On May 22, Nasser blocked the Gulf of Aqaba, a highly provocative action that effectively sealed off Israeli shipping from the Straits of Tiran. Israel interpreted this as a clear declaration of war and began to prepare accordingly. The Israeli government felt that Israel could not hope to fight a defensive war against several Arab states at once. Instead a lightning strike against Egypt and Syria was planned.

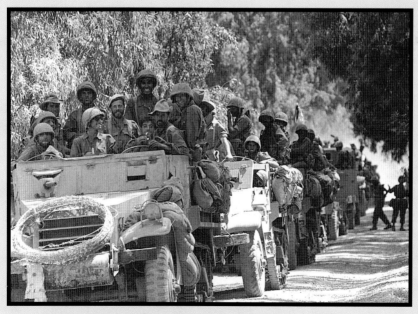

An Israeli column advances into Syria, June 1967.

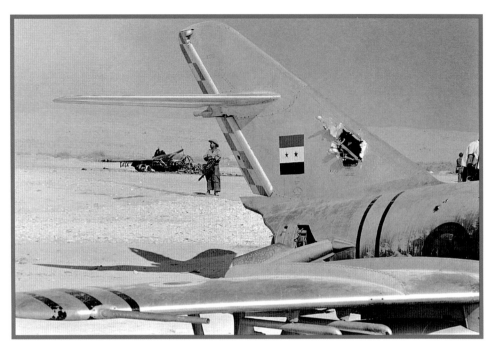

An Egyptian jet destroyed before it could take off. The speed of Israel's attack in 1967 stunned the Arab world.

Victory in Six Days

The war was a stunning triumph for the Israelis. It was effectively won on the day it began, and it seemed as though Nasser had neither the time nor the tactical know-how to manage any kind of adequate response. The entire operation went like clockwork and was flawlessly executed.

June 5, 1967

Israeli jets launched an early-morning attack on Egyptian air bases. They completely wiped out the Egyptian air defenses, destroying many planes before they could leave the ground. Later that day, in another round of attacks, they destroyed the Jordanian, Syrian, and Iraqi air forces. Things were now nicely in place for Israeli land forces to sweep with ease over the Sinai Desert. In a mere six days Egyptian troops had been forced back to the Suez Canal. Jerusalem and the West Bank were captured, and Israel seized the Golan Heights. By June 10, it was all over. The attack had been swift, ruthless, and expertly executed. The capture of Jerusalem was especially pleasing to the Israelis, leading Moshe Dayan, the Israeli defense minister, to declare: "We have returned home to this most sacred of shrines, never to part from it again."

Immediate Aftereffects

Arab prestige had been shattered by the nature of their defeat, while the Israelis were in a stronger position than ever before. They refused to withdraw from their newly acquired territories, the Golan Heights, the Sinai, the West Bank of the Jordan River, and the Gaza Strip. Conflict with Egypt continued in the Sinai area, but Israel's security was greatly increased. The Palestinians in the West Bank and Gaza found themselves back under Israeli control. To many of the refugees it was now clear that they could not rely on the Arab states to defeat Israel. Instead they would turn to the PLO as their only chance of liberation.

". . . no peace with Israel, no recognition of Israel, no negotiations with it, and insistence on the rights of the Palestinian people in their own country."
An extract from the Khartoum Declaration of September 1, 1967, in which the leaders of the Arab states affirmed their unity after the Six-Day War

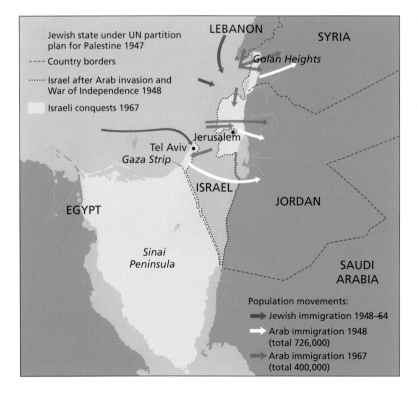

The map shows the changing face of the Middle East since World War II.

Turning Point: Yom Kippur War of 1973

In the years after the Six-Day War, there was continued fighting in Sinai between Israeli and Egyptian forces. Nasser hoped to wear down the Israelis slowly, forcing them to withdraw. The new prime minister of Israel, Golda Meir, retaliated, launching air strikes deep into Egyptian territory. Nasser was alarmed and sought help from the Soviet Union, which provided modern weapons in return for the use of Egyptian air and naval facilities. This placed the United States in a difficult position. Although supportive of Israel, it could not risk being dragged into a conflict in the Middle East that might involve the Soviet Union. American pressure forced Meir to call off the raids and enter into negotiations with Egypt in 1970.

Golda Meir addressing the world's press in London, 1970.

Anwar Sadat

During these negotiations President Nasser died, and was replaced by his deputy, Anwar Sadat. Sadat was willing to negotiate with both the United States and Israel, feeling that this was the best way to achieve the Egyptian goal of an Israeli withdrawal from the Sinai. Meir, on the other hand, felt that Israel's security depended on holding the Sinai and was unwilling to trade territory. In the years that followed, Sadat began to believe that only war would bring Israel to the negotiating table.

War Plans

Anwar Sadat knew that he could not risk war without the support of other Arab leaders, so he entered into talks with the new leader of Syria, President Hafiz al Assad. Syria also had a grudge against the Israelis and hoped to regain the Golan Heights, which it had lost in the 1967 war. The friendship between the two leaders was soon clear.

Israel ignored the warning signs, still confident of its own military strength after the easy victory of 1967. A complacent attitude prevailed in Israel, with many in the military regarding Arab forces as weak and disorganized. President Sadat was happy to encourage these feelings, emphasizing the poor condition of his army to Western journalists.

Yom Kippur

The Israelis were shaken out of their complacency when Egyptian and Syrian forces launched surprise attacks on October 6, 1973. The day was Yom Kippur, the holiest day of the Jewish people. Many soldiers were home on leave, weakening the Israeli defenses along the Suez Canal and in the Golan Heights. Egyptian tanks were able to overwhelm the Israeli forces and advance across the canal.

Weapons supplied by the USSR were crucial to the early Egyptian successes. When the Israeli air force tried to strike back, they were met with a barrage of Soviet-made ground-to-air missiles. In the north, the Syrians attacked with over a thousand tanks advancing into the Golan Heights.

Early Arab successes, however, could not be maintained. Israel was able quickly to move men, tanks, and equipment into the Sinai and strike back at the Egyptians. On October 14, 1973, the two nations fought the biggest tank battle of the 20th century in the Sinai desert. Over 250 Egyptian tanks were destroyed, against only ten Israeli tanks, allowing the Israelis to advance over the Suez Canal and threaten to encircle the Egyptian Third Army. Soviet spy satellites were able to detect this move and Sadat hastily began negotiations toward a ceasefire. When the ceasefire was called on October 22, it was swiftly broken by the Israelis who hoped to finish off the Third Army. The threat of full-scale Soviet involvement and pressure from the United States, however, forced an end to the conflict.

Results of the War

The Yom Kippur War showed clearly the central role played by both superpowers in the Middle East. The United States and USSR supplied the weaponry that enabled Israel and Egypt to fight battles on a massive scale. Both superpowers were anxious to end the conflict, America fearing a Soviet invasion, the Soviets recognizing that their ally, Egypt, faced defeat. The level of involvement was clearly illustrated when the United States went on a full nuclear alert, the highest stage of war readiness, when it heard of the Soviet threat to invade. This forced the USSR to drop its threat.

The Oil Weapon

Arab nations used their immense supplies of oil as a weapon and a bargaining chip to great advantage during the conflict. The Organization of the Petroleum Exporting Countries (OPEC) forced the price of oil up by over 70 percent and production was slowly reduced, threatening to starve the West of oil. Later in the year they raised prices by over 100 percent, forcing the West, in particular Great Britain and the United States, to adopt less pro-Israeli policies. Pressure from the West forced Israel to "disengage" from the Egyptian forces. They pulled back from their post-ceasefire positions and were replaced by United Nations troops. Realizing the potential of the oil weapon, the Arab nations began to show a new self-confidence in their dealings with Israel and the West.

Henry Kissinger, the U.S. secretary of state, arrives in Israel in October 1973. Superpower pressure was crucial to bringing the Yom Kippur conflict to an end.

Superpower involvement and the use of OPEC's "oil weapon" pressured Israel into taking part in peace talks with its Arab neighbors, eventually resulting in the Camp David Agreement (see pages 32–35).

The Yom Kippur War, although ultimately a military defeat for the Arabs, restored much of the pride that the Egyptians had lost during the 1967 war. President Assad of Syria announced soon afterward: *"... in those days of heroism, we corrected many mistaken ideas that were established about our nations. We have restored self-confidence to the Arab and we have proved to the enemy that our people are not the easy prey that the enemy thought."*

Drivers in Great Britain line up for gasoline in the 1973 fuel crisis following the Arab OPEC nations' use of oil as a bargaining tool in the conflict.

Turning Point: Camp David

The years following the Yom Kippur War of 1973 saw great changes in Middle Eastern politics. By 1977 Israel was in economic turmoil, with high inflation and political scandals rocking the left-wing Mapai government of Yitzhak Rabin.

In May 1977 the right wing Likud (Unity) party of Menachem Begin won most seats in a general election. Begin had been leader of the Irgun, a Jewish guerrilla group that had committed atrocities against Arabs during the 1948 war. With Begin in charge, a peace settlement seemed unlikely.

Pressure Mounts

In 1976 Jimmy Carter replaced Gerald Ford as president of the United States. He immediately made it clear that peace in the Middle East was an important priority. He met with the Syrian leader, President Assad, to encourage him to help negotiate a peace settlement that would settle the major issues of the region —the Golan Heights, the Sinai, the West Bank, and a homeland for the Palestinians. Assad, however, was eager to see the Palestinian areas become part of Syria, so he was unwilling to push for the negotiations urged by President Carter. Begin also seemed unlikely to support it, instead encouraging Jewish settlement of the West Bank.

The situation appeared deadlocked, but President Sadat was anxious that Egypt, not Syria, should lead the Arab world. In November 1977 he offered to become the first Arab leader to travel to Israel for talks. Although suspicious, Begin could not afford to risk angering the United States, so he accepted the offer.

Sadat in the Knesset

On November 20, President Sadat made a historic speech in the Knesset, the Israeli parliament. He offered a peace agreement between Israel and Egypt that would deal with the land gained by Israel in the 1967 war and the issue of a Palestinian homeland. Other Arab nations were furious. In traveling to Israel Sadat had given recognition to the existence of the State of Israel. He was now offering a separate peace, which would undermine Arab unity.

Camp David

In July 1978 Begin and Sadat met with President Carter at Camp David in Maryland. Secret talks followed, aimed at solving the problems of Israel's occupation of Sinai and the West Bank. Two documents emerged. In "The Framework for a Peace Treaty," Israel agreed to return the Sinai to Egyptian control over a three-year period in return for the reopening of the Suez Canal and Straits of Tiran to Israeli shipping. In the second document, "The Framework for Peace," Begin agreed to hold talks about the future of Gaza and the West Bank, aimed at some form of Palestinian self-government within five years. The second framework was very vague; Egypt was in no position to negotiate on behalf of the Palestinians or other Arab states, and in the end nothing came of its proposals.

Profile: Anwar Sadat 1918–1981

Anwar Sadat came from a peasant background but he was able to rise to become an army officer. His intense hatred of British involvement in Egypt led to his being imprisoned for links with the Nazis during World War II. He returned to the army in 1950 and joined in Nasser's revolt, overthrowing the corrupt regime of King Farouk. He held a variety of posts in Nasser's government, before succeeding him as president of Egypt in 1970. After Egypt's failure in the Yom Kippur War, he lessened the country's dependence on the USSR and began to cooperate more with the United States. In 1977 he bravely visited Israel, pressuring the Israeli prime minister, Menachem Begin, into taking part in the Camp David peace talks. As a result of this move, and his more pro-western approach, he was attacked by other Arab nations and militant Islamic groups in Egypt. He was assassinated in 1981.

A historic moment: Camp David, September 1978. President Sadat of Egypt (left) and Israeli prime minister Menachem Begin shake hands, with U.S. president Jimmy Carter looking on.

Results of Camp David

On his return from the United States, Begin successfully persuaded the Knesset to withdraw Israeli troops and settlers from the Sinai Peninsula, making a peace treaty possible. The two leaders returned to Camp David, signing a historic peace treaty on March 26, 1979.

The Camp David Agreement was the first peace treaty signed between Israel and an Arab state, bringing an end to thirty years of conflict with Egypt. Israel began to withdraw from the Sinai in May 1979, completing its withdrawal in 1982, and Begin and Sadat were awarded the Nobel Peace Prize.

The other Arab countries, however, were furious. In signing a separate peace treaty, Sadat had weakened the position of Arab states that still aimed for the destruction of Israel. His opposition to Islamic **fundamentalist** groups both inside and outside Egypt placed him under greater pressure. On October 6, 1981, attending a parade to mark the anniversary of the Yom Kippur War, Sadat was assassinated by members of an extremist group.

Paying the Price

In signing the Camp David Agreement Sadat not only helped bring peace between Egypt and Israel, he also effectively signed his own death warrant. Soon after the agreement the Syrian government proclaimed:

"He (Sadat) shed all respect when he stood in Jerusalem and saluted the Israeli flag and leaders and bowed . . . . Sadat is a cheap example of treachery . . . (his) end will be like that of other traitors."

Two years later he was assassinated.

Profile: Menachem Begin (1913–1992)

Originally from Russia, Begin became involved in **Zionist** youth movements at the age of 16. After spending time in concentration camps in the Soviet Union, Begin was able to escape to Palestine where he assumed command of the Irgun in 1943. He was to play a major role in the struggle for independence both before and after the British withdrawal, including the massacre at Deir Yassin in 1948.

After Israel gained independence Begin formed the Herut (Freedom) party and was elected to Israel's parliament, the Knesset. The Herut, which later combined with other right-wing parties to form the Likud (Unity) group, adopted a strongly nationalist line, advocating seizing further territory on both banks of the Jordan River. During the Six-Day War his hard-line views became more acceptable to his countrymen, eventually allowing him to become prime minister in 1977. He was the first Israeli leader to meet with the head of an Arab state that year, as he began talks with Anwar Sadat. The resulting Camp David accords led to the two being awarded the Nobel Peace Prize. Nevertheless he was still prepared to take strong action to defend Israel, and he authorized the invasion of Lebanon in 1982, before resigning as prime minister in 1983.

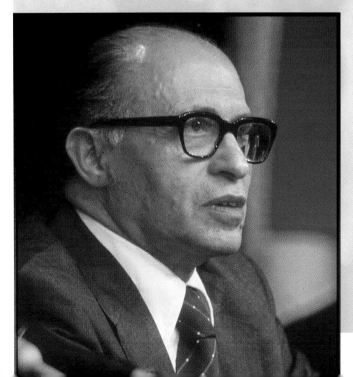

Menachem Begin, prime minister of Israel until 1983.

Turning Point: War in Lebanon

Lebanon, a small country to the north of Israel, became independent in 1945. Its people were divided fairly evenly between Muslims and Christians, until the 1948 war brought 100,000 Palestinian refugees into the country. By 1970 this figure had risen to 300,000, a tenth of the country's population. Each new phase of the Arab-Israeli conflict created division between Muslims and Christians in the country, threatening its newfound prosperity.

The Arrival of the PLO

The Six-Day War of 1967 drove thousands of Palestinian refugees out of the West Bank area, many making their way to Lebanon. Along with the refugees came members of the PLO who, from 1968 onward, began using Lebanon as a base for launching attacks on Israel. This situation worsened in late 1970, when King Hussein expelled the PLO from Jordan. The PLO set up its new headquarters in Lebanon, making it increasingly difficult for the Lebanese army to limit PLO operations. The Fedayeen assaults into Israel increased, resulting in Israeli reprisals in Lebanon in the form of air strikes and commando raids. The fragile peace between Lebanese Christians and Muslims was stretched to breaking point.

Beirut, August 28, 1982. A young PLO fighter is seen off by Yasir Arafat, as the PLO begin their withdrawal from Lebanon.

Israeli artillery on the attack in south Lebanon.

Civil War

The arrival of the PLO had heightened tension in Lebanon, and its decision to support the Muslim groups hastened the outbreak of a civil war. From 1975 on, Christian groups such as the Phalangist and Tiger militias fought Shiite and Druze Muslim militias, who were allied with the PLO. Some 40,000 people died and large areas of Beirut, the once-prosperous capital, were destroyed. It was unlikely that Lebanon's two powerful neighbors, Israel and Syria, would sit idly by and watch as the country disintegrated. Syria wanted to bring Lebanon under its influence, supporting the PLO and the Muslim militias while at the same time preventing them from becoming too independent of Syrian influence. Israel, meanwhile, looked to build an ally in a Christian government that would presumably clamp down on the PLO and Muslim extremist groups.

Israel Intervenes

Palestinian guerrillas staging raids on Israel from Lebanese territory in turn drew Israeli raids on Lebanon, as well as two large-scale Israeli invasions. In March 1978 the Israelis invaded south Lebanon in an attempt to create a "buffer zone" to lessen the impact of PLO attacks. They withdrew in June after the UN Security Council created a 6,000-man peacekeeping force for the area, called UNIFIL. The Israelis had organized a Christian militia designed to prevent PLO attacks across the border. As the Israelis departed from Lebanon, they turned over their strongholds in the south to this militia instead of to the UN forces.

The second Israeli invasion took place on June 6, 1982, after an assassination attempt by Palestinian terrorists on the Israeli ambassador in London. More than 170,000 heavily armed troops advanced deep into Lebanese territory, launching air strikes against PLO strongholds in residential areas of Beirut. They began to pull back their forces after a U.S. envoy successfully negotiated the withdrawal of most of the PLO to other Arab nations.

Massacre at Sabra-Chatila

The violence seemed to have come to an end when, on September 14, Bashir Gemayel, the 34-year-old president-elect of Lebanon, was killed by a bomb that destroyed the headquarters of his Christian Phalangist party. The day after the assassination, Israeli troops moved into West Beirut in force. They surrounded the Sabra-Chatila refugee camps, claiming that PLO guerrillas were using them as cover. In September 1982 the Israeli military, under the command of Ariel Sharon, allowed Christian militiamen to search the camps, resulting in the massacre of Palestinians there. Israel denied responsibility, but the massacre turned many Israelis against the war. The effects and repercussions of these events are discussed on pages 45–46.

Israel Withdraws

Israeli forces began to withdraw their forces from Lebanon in 1983 and were replaced by a multinational peacekeeping force composed of U.S. marines and British, French, and Italian soldiers. Their mandate was to support the central Lebanese government, but they soon found themselves drawn into the struggle for power between different Lebanese factions. During their stay in Lebanon, 260 U.S. marines and about 60 French soldiers were killed, most of them in suicide bombings of the marine and French army compounds on October 23, 1983. The multinational force left in the spring of 1984. The retreating Israeli forces also came under attack from Shiite suicide bombers. The Israelis eventually left Lebanon in 1985, although they maintained a presence in the south to provide Israel with a "security zone."

U.S. marines search for the victims of the suicide bombing of their base in Beirut.

Continued Conflict

The withdrawal of the bulk of Israel's forces did not bring peace to Lebanon. In July 1986, Syrian observers took up a position in Beirut to monitor a peacekeeping agreement. The agreement soon broke down; fighting between Shiite and Druze militia in West Beirut became so intense that Syrian troops moved in in force in February 1987, suppressing militia resistance. Hostage taking of American and British citizens became commonplace, as Muslim militias tried to highlight their grievances. Meanwhile the PLO continued to make raids across the border into Israel. They were joined by a new extremist group, Hezbollah (Party of God), which was supported by Iran and Syria. Meanwhile, Christian forces, especially those led by General Michael Aoun, continued their "war of liberation" against Syria.

Search for a Settlement

The beginning of the end of the war came when Lebanon's leaders met in Taif, Saudi Arabia, in October 1989. There they formulated the Taif Agreement for a National Reconciliation Charter, which was approved on November 4. A new president, René Moawad, was elected but was assassinated only 17 days later. His replacement, Elias Hrawi, put down the rebellion of his fellow Christian, General Aoun, who was forced to flee to France. The fighting over, the new Government of National Reconciliation began the delicate task of disarming the militias and restoring stability. In a decade and a half of war, an estimated 130,000 to 150,000 people were killed and thousands more wounded.

Although the civil war had been brought to an end, some militia groups remained active. The Christian South Lebanese Army (SLA) refused to disband, and Hezbollah continued to attack Israeli territory. As a result, Israel refused to withdraw from southern Lebanon and launched reprisal attacks against Hezbollah strongholds throughout the 1990s. In 1996 the United States negotiated a truce whereby Hezbollah agreed not to attack Israeli territory, but it was accepted that they could resist the Israeli forces in the "security zone." This, along with the eventual collapse of their Christian allies the SLA, forced the Israelis to act. In March 2000 the Knesset voted to withdraw all Israeli forces in southern Lebanon. The last troops left on May 24. The following day the Lebanese government declared an annual public holiday, to be called "Resistance and Liberation Day."

A Global Conflict

The conflict between Israel and its Arab neighbors in the 1960s and 70s saw the emergence of many guerrilla and militia groups. While making peace with Egypt, the Israelis found themselves under attack from Fatah, the armed wing of the PLO. Fatah operated from the West Bank area, Jordan, and Lebanon, carrying out bombings in Israel itself and engaging in gun battles with Israeli troops. Between 1967 and 1970, Fatah attacks claimed the lives of more Israeli troops than had been killed in the Six-Day War: more than 500, as well as 116 **civilians**.

However, throughout the 1970s it became clear to many Palestinian supporters that they could neither hope to defeat the Israelis by themselves nor rely on Arab states to do it for them. Some Arab states, particularly Egypt, seemed to be coming to terms with their Israeli neighbors, making some Palestinians feel that their cause was being sidelined.

The Extension of the Conflict

In the early 1970s new Palestinian groups emerged, determined that world opinion would not forget about their cause. These new groups, such as the Popular Front for the Liberation of Palestine (PFLP) and Black September, were prepared to use extreme methods.

The PFLP organized a series of airplane hijackings that resulted in many deaths but attracted the attention of the world's media. In one of the most spectacular PFLP attacks, three airliners were forced to fly to an airstrip in Jordan. Some 600 passengers were held hostage, with the PFLP demanding the release from prison of one of their members. When the British government released the hijacker, the passengers were freed before the three planes were blown apart in full view of the world's press.

Black September

The PFLP hijacking forced King Hussein of Jordan to take action against the PLO in his own country. In September 1970 the Jordanian army expelled the PLO, forcing them to retreat into Syria and Lebanon. Palestinians called the expulsion "Black September," a name also adopted by a new guerrilla group. In 1971 they assassinated the prime minister of Jordan in revenge for events of the previous year. The following year Black September carried out their most infamous action. They kidnapped 11 Israeli athletes who were taking part in the 1972

The Olympic flag flies at half mast as crowds attend a memorial service for the Israeli athletes killed by Arab terrorists.

Olympics in Munich, Germany. A gun battle with police followed in which all 11 hostages were killed, as well as five members of Black September. World public opinion was shocked by the attack—the Olympic Games were regarded as a bastion of peace, free from politics—but once again the Palestinian cause was front-page news.

Raid on Entebbe

In the late 1970s Palestinian groups began to reject hijacking as a means of attracting publicity. This was partly in response to an unsuccessful hijacking in 1976. Four terrorists had ordered a plane carrying more than 200 passengers from Israel to France to land instead at Entebbe in Uganda. The 110 Israeli passengers on board were held hostage. The terrorists demanded that 53 Palestinians be released from jails in Europe and Israel. Instead of meeting their demands, the Israelis flew a group of commandos 2,500 miles to Uganda. Under cover of darkness they burst into the airport building and killed all the terrorists, taking just 45 seconds to carry out their mission. It was now clear to terrorists backing the Palestinians that Israel was prepared to go to great lengths to defend its people.

America Becomes a Target

The decline in hijacking, however, was only a change in tactics, not an end to terrorist attacks. The 1982 invasion of Lebanon led to the rise of other groups determined to strike back at Israel and its allies. Increasingly, some fundamentalist Islamic states, such as Iran and Libya, began to regard the United States as an enemy of the Arab people. To such nations the United States was the main ally of Israel, its main source of weapons, and its diplomatic support in the UN. The targeting of American troops and civilians became common, as Arab groups tried to publicize their cause and force a change in U.S. government policy.

In 1983 a Shiite militia called Amal was set up in Lebanon, intent on forcing the Israelis and the U.S. peacekeepers out of the country. In April of that year one of its members drove a truckload of explosives into the American Embassy compound in Beirut, killing 63 people. Later in the year another suicide bomber drove into the U.S. marine base. In the resulting explosion 219 people were killed and 75 injured. It was clear to U.S. president Ronald Reagan that he had a stark choice—withdraw from Lebanon or face an all-out war with Amal and its Syrian backers. In February 1984 he ordered a withdrawal, but the United States has remained a target for Islamic fundamentalists, and occasionally it has struck back.

Crash investigators in Lockerbie search for evidence around the remains of the cockpit of Pan Am flight 103, December 23, 1988.

Libya and the United States

In 1969 a group of army officers led by Colonel Muammar al Qaddafi seized power in the north African state of Libya. Qaddafi was a devout follower of Islam and hoped that he and his country could play a dominant role in Arab affairs.

He soon made his hatred of the western powers clear, offering support to terrorist groups willing to strike at countries such as the United States and Great Britain. Money and weapons were provided for groups such as the PLO and the IRA (Irish Republican Army), and soon a diverse range of left-wing and Islamic terrorist groups were looking to Qaddafi for support.

The regime was believed to be linked to a series of assassinations and terrorist activities. Tensions between Libya and the United States rose in 1981 when U.S. navy jets shot down two Libyan planes. In 1986, responding to heightened terrorism apparently directed by Libya against Americans in Europe, the United States bombed sites in Libya declared by President Reagan to be "terrorist centers," including Tripoli, the capital city, and Qaddafi's residential compound. Several dozen Libyans died in the attack, including Qaddafi's 2-year-old adopted daughter.

Two years later Arab bombers struck. A total of 270 people died when Pan Am flight 103 was blown out of the sky over Lockerbie, Scotland, on December 21, 1988. It was the worst act of airline terrorism against the United States up to that time. It has also been called the world's biggest unsolved murder.

Although some observers believe that either Syria or Iran was involved, the United States accused Libya of harboring the bombers. In 1992 the UN introduced **sanctions** against Libya, and a prolonged campaign for **extradition** of the suspected bombers followed. After extensive negotiations Qaddafi conceded that the two suspects could be put on trial in the Netherlands, a neutral site, in May 2000. One was found guilty and sentenced to life in prison, while the other was acquitted.

The Media and the Conflict

The media, both within the Middle East and around the globe, have had an important role to play in the 55 years of tension and war between Israel and her neighbors. Inevitably over these years, there have been many changes in the media's perception of the conflict. The importance of the region has ensured that the international media kept a close eye on political developments, while in Israel and the Arab states the media have been central to the promotion of both peace and war.

Palestinian women fighting Israeli soldiers in Ramallah, 1988, during the first Intifada

Early Years of the Conflict

The state of Israel was born in the turbulent years that followed World War II. In Great Britain the public yearned for peace, so stories of British soldiers dying in Palestine soon forced the government to hand over control of the area to the UN. Images of the Nazi Holocaust were still fresh in the minds of many in the West, and public sympathy was very much with the Jews. Images of Jewish refugees from the Holocaust being turned away by British warships as they approached Palestine shocked the world.

The propaganda effect of the ships decked with British flags daubed with Nazi swastikas forced a change in government policy, allowing more Jewish refugees into Palestine. The media had been central to the creation of Israel and would later play an important role in forcing the British to climb down during the Suez Crisis. The importance of the media in shaping world opinion and government policies toward the Middle East was clear.

The Media's Role in the Six-Day War of 1967

In the buildup to the Six-Day War, the media in some Arab states helped whip their readers and listeners into frenzy, encouraging them to expect a swift and glorious victory. Cartoons in Egyptian and Lebanese newspapers portrayed Israel as a weak nation surrounded by more powerful Arab enemies. In May, Cairo Radio declared: "It is our chance, Arabs, to direct a blow of death and annihilation to Israel and all its presence in our Holy Land." The defeat that followed stunned the Arab world, and its media were forced to accept their role in raising expectations. The Egyptian magazine *Al-Mussawar* admitted encouraging Egypt's government to adopt an aggressive position: "We have been saying things that we did not always mean … the main influence was on the Arabs; it raised their expectations to a point where promises had to be fulfilled."

Israel's First Defeat: Lebanon

Until the 1982 invasion of Lebanon, the Israeli media had generally been supportive of the government's strong line with its Arab neighbors. The world's press, while concerned at the ongoing conflict, had also broadly accepted the view that it was Arab states, not Israel, that were the aggressors in the region. Events in Lebanon changed that perception, and Israel found itself under fire both at home and abroad.

The massacre of Palestinian refugees in the Sabra-Chatila camps stunned the world. The Israeli government tried to wash its hands of the crime, blaming the Christian Phalangists. Menachem Begin made his government's position clear: "Non-Jews kill non-Jews—and the world wants to hang Israel for the crime." Israeli sympathizers took out advertisements in the American press, claiming that the Israeli army could have done nothing to prevent the massacres.

Criticism nevertheless grew: although the Israeli army had not taken part, they had stood by as their allies carried out the killings, in some cases within earshot of the cries of the victims. For the first time the Israeli press began to criticize government defense policy. One journalist, comparing the massacres to Nazi atrocities committed against the Jews, wrote: "We shall never be able to cleanse ourselves of this stain."

Media pressure at home and abroad grew, and 400,000 people took part in an anti-war demonstration in Tel Aviv. Israeli defense minister Ariel Sharon resigned, and Israel was forced to withdraw from Lebanon the following year. Media pressure had again influenced events in the region.

Global Terrorism

The pro-Palestinian and Islamic fundamentalist terror groups that emerged in the 1970s were eager to exploit the media to promote their cause. After the hijacking of three aircraft in 1970, the leader of the PFLP, George Habash, made clear the importance of attracting media attention: "For decades world public opinion has been neither for or against the Palestinians. At least the world is talking about us now." The killing of 11 Israeli athletes in 1972 achieved the same goal. Later Lebanese Islamic groups adopted a new tactic. Western civilians working in Beirut were taken hostage and held for long periods in harsh conditions, their plight calling attention to the cause of the kidnappers. However, the publicity generated by such actions, while gaining exposure, did little to attract international sympathy to the Arab cause.

Terry Waite, the Archbishop of Canterbury's envoy, was kidnapped by Shiite Muslims in 1987 and held hostage in Beirut until 1991.

In the United States in particular, some Arab nations (notably Libya) and terrorist groups have become the cause of much popular fear and hatred. Since the collapse of the Soviet Union, fear of nuclear attack from "rogue Arab states" has replaced the communist threat. Increasingly this is reflected in the popular media, as Hollywood movies replace Soviet villain figures with militant Arab terrorists. The U.S. media have been heavily committed to the support of Israel, forcing politicians to adopt a similar attitude or risk attack from the press.

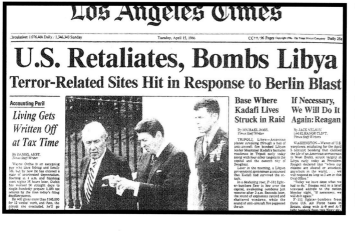

The *Los Angeles Times*, April 15, 1986. The U.S. media were strongly supportive of President Ronald Reagan's retaliation for an earlier bombing in which an American serviceman was killed.

The Intifada

It was not until 1987 that a new Palestinian movement was able to attract widespread public sympathy. When the young people of the West Bank rose up in the Intifada, Israel did not know how to react. It was difficult to denounce such a popular and uncoordinated movement as the work of "terrorists." Despite the hard-line "iron-fist" policy, in which he famously advised the security forces to "break the bones of the rioters," defense minister Yitzhak Rabin prevailed. However, with every televised incident of Israel's heavy-handed response, the Palestinians rose in international stature while the Israelis lost more and more credibility. The casualties were high. Some 1,300 Palestinians, including 300 children, were killed, but the popular unrest and its coverage had stunned the international community. The need for a permanent solution appeared more important than ever.

The international media had again played an important role in pressing for a peaceful solution to the conflict. The images of the Intifada were a crucial factor in pushing the Israeli government into engaging in peace talks. In addition, the PLO gained publicity without using terrorist attacks.

Turning Point: Hopes for Peace

On December 9, 1987, the uprising called the Intifada erupted. This outbreak of violence, with images of confrontations between stone-throwing Arab youths and the Israeli army flashing around the world, helped lead to the PLO's recognition of Israel and hope for some kind of peace settlement.

The Intifada. Images of poorly equipped Palestinian youths clashing with the Israeli army shocked the world.

The Intifada

The first demonstrations and clashes were not the responsibility of the PLO but were a response to the continued Israeli occupation of Gaza and the West Bank. Militant religious groups, such as Islamic Jihad and HAMAS, helped turn this frustration into direct action.

The spread of the rebellion into Israel itself alarmed the Israelis. The reaction of the Israeli army was swift and decisive. Yitzhak Rabin (defense minister in a **coalition** government) announced an "iron-fist" policy, ordering his soldiers to use live ammunition against the rioters. However, the violence of the army was counterproductive. Their actions, broadcast on news bulletins around the world, brought international condemnation.

Usually a reliable ally of Israel, the United States joined in the criticism. Israeli prime minister Yitzhak Shamir refused to be swayed by international opinion, but it was becoming clear that efforts to end the unrest using the military were failing.

Some form of Palestinian self-rule seemed the only possible solution. U.S. secretary of state George Schultz set out a peace plan in February 1988. Foreign minister Shimon Peres, leader of the Labor Party in the governing coalition, backed the plan, but Shamir remained firmly opposed along with the majority of Israel's Jewish population. The plan stalled and the Intifada intensified.

PLO Recognizes Israel

Attention now turned to the question of whether the PLO, as the representative of the Palestinian people, was prepared to recognize the state of Israel. The Palestinian National Charter of July 1968 had declared Palestine to be their homeland and had called for armed struggle to secure the "elimination of Zionism in Palestine." This objective, translated in many minds as "the destruction of Israel," seemed to be confirmed by the actions of the PLO in the years that followed. Why should the PLO now change its mind?

The Effects of the Intifada

The Intifada had not only placed the issue of the Middle East in the forefront of world attention, it had also aroused a wave of international sympathy for the Palestinian cause along with a feeling that something should be done. However, as the failure of the Intifada had shown, Israel could not be removed from the Occupied Territories by Palestinian action alone. Israel had a firm policy of refusing to talk with the PLO, which it regarded as a terrorist organization. For the Palestinians to make any progress, it was necessary to enlist the aid of the world's major powers. The Soviet Union was preoccupied with its own internal problems, so it was to the West, and principally the United States, that the Palestinians had to turn if they wanted assistance.

The Americans, however, had promised that they would not talk to the PLO until the PLO recognized the state of Israel and its right to exist, and renounced the use of terrorism.

Steps to Recognition

Through the closing months of 1988 intense diplomatic activity led to a series of meetings as the PLO tried to make its policies more acceptable to the United States. The most notable steps were:

- November 5—The Palestinian National Council declared a Palestinian state, with Jerusalem as its capital. It also proclaimed its acceptance of UN resolutions 242 and 338 that recognize Israel's right to exist.
- December 13—Arafat spoke to the United Nations General Assembly in Geneva.
- December 14—At a specially convened press conference Arafat affirmed Israel's right to exist in peace and security and added: "We totally and absolutely renounce all forms of terrorism."

Within four hours of this pronouncement, American secretary of state George Schultz announced that the United States would open negotiations with the PLO. The Israelis were furious.

The Gulf War

The Iraqi invasion of Kuwait in August 1990 would become a crucial matter in the peace process. The Iraqis found themselves under immense pressure to withdraw, but their leader, Saddam Hussein, steadfastly refused. He argued that if the UN demanded the withdrawal of his troops from Kuwait, they must do the same with Israeli forces in Lebanon. The PLO announced that they backed Iraq, and there was some sympathy in Arab nations. Despite this, a U.S.-led coalition launched an attack on January 17, 1991, backed by several states. The war lasted only 43 days and ended in Iraq's withdrawal from Kuwait.

Peace Talks Begin

Iraq's defeat in the Gulf War put the PLO under great pressure. Iraq had been a major financial backer of the PLO, as were several of the Arab Gulf states that supported the U.S. coalition. The possible threat to their financial support convinced many in the PLO to adopt a more positive approach to talks with Israel. In November 1991 peace talks between the Israelis, the Arab nations, and the Palestinians were held in Madrid. Under the spotlight of the world's media, little was achieved.

The Oslo Accords

In the 1992 Israeli elections, Yikzhak Rabin's Labor Party had defeated Shamir's right-wing coalition. Rabin, who had ordered the "iron-fist" policy at the onset of the Intifada, had since realized that force could not subdue the uprising. He also recognized that the Jewish population of Israel would soon be surpassed by the substantially higher birth rate of the Palestinians. Arafat appeared to be leading the PLO toward more moderate policies, so the time seemed right for negotiations.

Beginning in January 1993 secret talks were held in Oslo, eventually resulting in the Oslo Accords. On September 13 in Washington, an agreement was formally signed by Rabin, Arafat, and President Clinton, and appeared to offer fresh hope to the troubled region.

Israeli prime minister Yitzhak Rabin signs the Washington Agreement that formally ratifies the Oslo Accords. Behind him U.S. president Bill Clinton and Yasir Arafat of the PLO look on.

The Main Terms of the Oslo Accords:

- Israel would withdraw from the Occupied Territories of the Gaza Strip and Jericho, allowing the Palestinians to take over their administration. Soon after, the Palestinians would become responsible for the security of the two areas, as well.
- Jewish settlers would remain in the territories, but would come under Israeli jurisdiction.
- After two years the negotiations would move on to a second phase, when issues such as the future of Jerusalem and Israeli settlements would be discussed.

A False Dawn?

The Oslo Accords and the historic handshake between Rabin and Arafat on the White House lawn appeared to offer new hope for peace in the Middle East, but obstacles remained. As a result of the angry reaction from extremists both within Israel and among the Palestinians, negotiations after Oslo took place against a background of violence.

Massacre at Hebron—End of the Intifada

The peace process seemed doomed early in 1994, when events in the West Bank town of Hebron threatened to shatter the fragile accord between Rabin and Arafat. The area around Hebron contained many Jewish settlers, and one village, Kiryat Arba, had become a center for Jewish extremism.

On February 25 an immigrant from New York, Dr. Bernard Goldstein, entered the Tomb of the Patriarchs in Hebron, a holy site for both Muslims and Jews. He opened fire on a crowd of praying Muslims, killing 29 people before being overcome. His act sparked Palestinian violence throughout the West Bank and security force reprisals, but he was hailed as a hero among right-wing Jewish groups.

Israeli settlers protest in the West Bank.

In spite of the growing unrest, Arafat and Rabin pressed on. In May 1994 they reached agreement in Cairo, setting out the terms for Palestinian self-rule. Soon after, Israeli troops began to withdraw and the Intifada ground to a halt. Later that year a historic peace treaty was signed between Israel and Jordan, the first between Israel and an Arab state since the 1979 Camp David Agreement. Following Jordan's lead, other Arab states began to open up diplomatic relations with Israel.

Violence and Assassination

The implementation of the Oslo Accords soon brought a further upsurge in violence, as extremists on both sides put pressure on their leaders. A new Palestinian group—HAMAS—had emerged in the Occupied Territories during the Intifada, unhappy with Arafat's increasingly moderate policies. In 1994 it began a bombing campaign in Israel and gained further publicity when it kidnapped and killed an Israeli soldier.

This murder coincided with the awarding of the Nobel Peace Prize to Rabin, Arafat, and Peres, and brought calls for tighter security from many in Israel. Rabin warned that if the Palestinians did not subdue HAMAS, then further self-rule was out of the question. Arafat was placed in a difficult position. His leadership was increasingly questioned as the new **Palestinian National Authority** attempted to control HAMAS while the Israelis expanded their settlements around Jerusalem.

Despite this pressure September 1995 saw an agreement to extend Palestinian self-rule, closely followed by elections in Gaza, Jericho, and the West Bank. This was the final straw for some right-wing Israelis. Yitzhak Rabin had been bearing the brunt of their anger. Rallies around Israel declared him a traitor, and some rabbis were calling for his death. On November 4 he was gunned down by a Jewish extremist, after addressing 100,000 people at a peace rally in Tel Aviv.

Rabin's assassination called into question the survival of the Peace Process. Shimon Peres, his successor as prime minister, did not hold the same respect among the more militant voters in Israel. Israeli support for the peace process would be severely tested in the November 1996 elections.

The Election of Netanyahu

The 1996 Israeli general election took place in an atmosphere of rising tension. Shimon Peres moved the election to May in the hope that he could exploit the revulsion at the death of Rabin. However, a HAMAS bombing campaign brought an increasing number of Israeli voters behind Benjamin Netanyahu's right-wing Likud party. Netanyahu narrowly won the election, promising to improve security and adopt a strong line with the Palestinians. His right-wing coalition included extreme Orthodox groups who were unlikely to accept movement in the peace process.

Netanyahu soon made his policies clear. The Jewish settlement program was expanded and he refused to meet Arafat, who in turn came under increasing pressure as his moderate policies began to falter. In September 1996 HAMAS violence intensified, when Netanyahu authorized the archaeological excavation of an ancient tunnel close to the Dome of the Rock in Jerusalem, an important Muslim site. It seemed as if the peace process had again reached a dead end.

Profile: Yitzhak Rabin (1922–1995)

Yitzhak Rabin was born in Jerusalem during the time of the British Mandate, becoming a member of a Haganah commando unit during World War II. After a brief period of imprisonment under the British, he fought in the 1948 War of Independence before rising rapidly through the ranks of the Israeli army to become its commander in 1964. In this position he led the army in the 1967 Six-Day War, becoming a national hero. In 1974 he replaced Golda Meir as leader of the Labor Party and became the first Israeli prime minister who had been born in the new state. After electoral defeat in 1977 he held a number of coalition government positions, until again becoming prime minister in 1992. His efforts to reach peace with the Palestinians led to the Oslo Accords in 1993 and the Nobel Peace Prize in 1994. The following year he was assassinated, robbing Israel of a forceful champion of peace.

The coffin of Yitzhak Rabin is carried to Mount Herzl cemetery, November 6, 1995.

The Hebron and Wye River Agreements

The 1993 Oslo Accords prescribed that Israel and the Palestinians would meet again within two years to discuss key issues. Instead, under Netanyahu, little was achieved other than protracted negotiations over how to put the Oslo Accords into effect. In the Hebron agreement of January 1997, the Israelis agreed to withdraw from 80 percent of that city, leaving a substantial force to protect the 400 Jewish settlers. In October 1998 the Wye River Agreement saw the Israelis agreeing to withdraw from a further 13.1 percent of the West Bank and to allow movement between the Gaza Strip and the other Palestinian areas. They agreed, as well, to release 2,000 Palestinian prisoners. In return, Arafat agreed to crack down on HAMAS with advice from American security experts. However, little was achieved by these agreements; to many Palestinians all of the Occupied Territories should be handed over, not a mere 13 percent, while to right-wing Israelis Netanyahu was going too far.

Israeli prime minister Benjamin Netanyahu meets PLO leader Yasir Arafat for the first time, September 4, 1996. Despite such meetings the peace process continued to slow down after the assassination of Rabin.

The Election of Ehud Barak and a Camp David Meeting

In July 1999, Netanyahu was defeated in an Israeli general election. His successor, Ehud Barak, led a left-of-center group called the One Israel Coalition. As Israel's most decorated soldier it was felt that he might be more likely to win the support of hardliners for a peace deal, so when he met with Arafat at Camp David in July 2000 hopes were high. However, it soon became clear that neither side was going to be able to reach a compromise. Barak's fragile coalition in the Knesset would not allow compromise on control of Jerusalem. Arafat, meanwhile, was unwilling to negotiate an agreement that avoided tackling the status of Jerusalem, fearing violence in the Palestinian territories. Although both sides continued to proclaim their desire to achieve a settlement that would bring lasting peace to the Middle East, the talks broke down.

Peace Shattered

Doubts about the talks at Camp David and the uncertain status of Jerusalem were justified within a few months. In late September 2000, violence erupted in Gaza and the West Bank after Israel's right-wing opposition leader Ariel Sharon led a delegation from his party to the place in Jerusalem that Jews call the Temple Mount. Muslims call the site Haram al-Sharif, or Noble Sanctuary. The control of this site, sacred to both religions, is a crucial flashpoint in the peace process.

Sharon's provocative visit ignited the passions on each side of the conflict. Palestinian crowds attacked Israeli security forces with stones and gunfire. The Israeli response was swift and deadly. Attacks by helicopter gunships and troops firing live ammunition left more than 100 Palestinians dead or wounded in the weeks of confrontation.

The years of peace talks seemed to have been forgotten as stories emerged of brutality on both sides. Two Israeli soldiers were beaten to death by a Palestinian mob in Ramallah in the West Bank. The Israeli army retaliated with rocket attacks on the city. Each side blamed the other for the violence.

Fighting continues in the West Bank, 2000.

International Fears

The international community was in no doubt that the fragile peace process had been shattered, possibly permanently, by the worst violence since 1996. The price of oil soared, an indication of the tension in the Arab world. The United Nations condemned Israel's attacks, which many felt were excessive, although the United States opposed the vote. There were signs that the conflict could spread across the Middle East, when an American warship was attacked by Arab extremists in Yemen.

By early 2002, the situation had worsened. Barak had been replaced as prime minister of Israel by the most hawkish Israeli politician, former general and minister of defense Ariel Sharon. With President George Bush of the United States declaring a global "war on terror" in the aftermath of the September 11, 2001 terrorist attacks on the World Trade Center in New York City, Sharon felt he had the U.S. go-ahead to take a hard line against the PLO and HAMAS. Military incursions into territory ostensibly governed by the Palestinian National Authority followed.

The Palestinians responded with an unprecedented series of terrorist attacks within both the Occupied Territories and Israel proper. Most of these took the form of "suicide bombings," in which a young Palestinian detonated explosives strapped to his or her body, killing him- or herself and others within the vicinity. Holding Arafat responsible for the violence, Sharon declared Israel "at war" with the Palestinians. Arafat, Sharon said, was the "enemy of the entire free world." By April 2002, Arafat was trapped by Israeli military forces in three small rooms of the PLO compound in Ramallah. Peace in this western region once again seemed a very distant prospect.

The Future

Without agreement on some unresolved key issues, it is unlikely that any long-lasting peace can be achieved in the Middle East.

1 A Palestinian State

In Oslo it was agreed that Palestinians living in the West Bank and Gaza could have a limited form of self-rule, with overall sovereignty lying with Israel. Palestinian hopes for their own sovereign state was left for later talks.

The final borders of the Palestinian state were also undecided. The Palestinians expect that state to comprise all of the Palestinian territories conquered in 1967. They argue that, having accepted the principle of Palestinian statehood limited to the West Bank and Gaza, they cannot be expected to compromise further. The Israelis accept a Palestinian state, but are concerned about their security. The larger the Palestinian area, the easier it would be for other Arab states to use it as a base to attack Israel.

2 Israeli Settlements

Although the Occupied Territories never formally became part of Israel, tens of thousands of Israelis have settled on land taken from Palestinians. Today there are 155,000 Israeli settlers living in the West Bank and 6,000 in Gaza.

The Palestinians argue that Israeli settlements are illegal, and that the settlers have to be removed under any peace agreement. However, they have been forced to accept that some settlers will remain in small areas guarded by the Israeli military. These settlements remain flashpoints for violence between Israelis and Palestinians.

To the Israelis the settlers are important, especially since their towns and villages help provide a security presence throughout the West Bank. Right-wing groups in Israel would be furious if the settlers were "betrayed," which makes compromise difficult.

Innocent civilians, like Sami Abu Jazar, were caught in the fighting in 2000.

3 Jerusalem

The future of Jerusalem is one of the most emotional issues in the conflict and was a major sticking point in the Camp David talks. It is a holy site for both Judaism and Islam, but has been under Israeli control since the 1967 war.

The Palestinian position: The Palestinians call Jerusalem Al Quds and regard it as the capital of their future state. They want a division between Israeli and Arab sections, with access to religious sites guaranteed to both.

The Israeli position: Israel claims that Jerusalem is its "eternal" capital and that the city will remain undivided under Israeli control, although they do concede access to religious sites.

4 Water

The shortage of water in the Middle East makes its allocation a central issue. A Water Resources Working Group was set up by the Oslo agreement. Israel, Jordan, and the Palestinians were to try to work together to manage the demand for the region's diminishing water supplies.

The Palestinian position: Palestinians complain that many Palestinian houses are not connected to a water supply, while Israeli settlers draw unlimited water from West Bank sources.

The Israeli position: Israel will not easily give up its control of West Bank water sources or access to the Jordan River. There have already been disputes with Jordan over the allocation of water supplies from the Jordan River.

Hopes for Compromise

As the violence continues in the West Bank and Gaza, any settlement of the conflict seems unlikely, but there may be room for compromise. The issues of the Palestinian state and the settlers have already seen movement from both sides, while Israeli plans for an undersea water pipeline from Turkey may relieve tension over water supplies. The sticking point has been Jerusalem.

After fifty years of conflict, there are reasons for hope. Two peoples, who at one stage swore to wipe each other from the face of the earth, have engaged in negotiations, although decades of bitterness and the holiest city in the world stand in the way of a lasting settlement.

Timeline

1914–1918   World War I, with Great Britain fighting alongside Arabs against Turkey

1917   Balfour Declaration: Great Britain agrees to support a Jewish homeland in Palestine

1920   Control of Palestine given to Great Britain under a League of Nations mandate.
Jewish immigrants in Palestine begin to increase.

1936   Arab Revolt against Great Britain begins

1939   World War II begins.
Arab Revolt defeated.
Jewish immigration to Palestine is limited.

1944   Irgun terrorists begin attacks on British forces

1945   End of World War II

1946   Irgun bombs King David Hotel, British military headquarters, Palestine

1947   Great Britain announces plans to leave Palestine.
UN decides to partition Palestine.

1948   British leave Palestine.
State of Israel declared.
Five Arab states invade Israel but are defeated, leaving thousands of Palestinian Arabs as refugees.

1952   Nasser becomes leader of Egypt

1955   Palestinian Fedayeen begin raids into Israel

1956   Suez–Sinai war: Israel conquers the Sinai Peninsula but is forced to withdraw by UN the following year

1964   PLO set up

1967   Six-Day War: Israel conquers the Sinai, the Gaza strip, the West Bank, and the Golan Heights

1970   "Black September": King Hussein expels the PLO from Jordan.
Nasser dies; replaced by Sadat.

1972   Palestinians murder 11 Israeli athletes at the Munich Olympics

1973   Yom Kippur War.
First use of "oil weapon" by Arab states.

1975   Civil war begins in Lebanon

1976   Israel rescues 100 hostages in the Entebbe raid

1977   Begin becomes prime minister of Israel.
Egyptian President Sadat visits Israel.

1978   Camp David peace agreement between Israel and Egypt

1981   President Sadat assassinated

1982   Israelis withdraw from the Sinai.
Israel invades Lebanon.
PLO forced out of Beirut.
Christian militia members, watched by the Israelis, massacre Palestinian refugees in Sabra and Chatila camps.

1983   UN peacekeeping force arrives in Lebanon.
260 U.S. marines killed in a suicide bomb attack in Beirut.

1984   Peacekeeping force begins to leave Beirut

1985   Israel begins withdrawal from Lebanon.
Kidnapping tactic introduced by fundamentalists in Beirut.

1986   United States bombs sites in Libya

1987   Palestinian Intifada begins in the Occupied Territories

1988   King Hussein renounces Jordan's claim to the West Bank.
PLO formally recognizes state of Israel.
Lockerbie bomb.

1989   Taif Agreement brings an end to war in Lebanon

1990   Saddam Hussein's Iraq invades Kuwait; a U.S.-led coalition is set up to oppose him

1991   Iraq defeated in the Gulf War.
Talks between Israelis and Palestinians begin.

1992   Yitzhak Rabin elected Israeli prime minister

1993 Oslo peace talks between Israel and PLO result in peace agreement being signed in Washington.
Hamas violence intensifies.

1994 Hebron Massacre.
Palestinian self-rule begins.
End of the Intifada.
Israel and Jordan sign a peace agreement.
Arafat, Rabin, and Peres awarded Nobel Peace Prize.

1995 Yitzhak Rabin assassinated

1996 Palestinian self-rule elections held with Arafat winning a landslide victory.
Netanyahu defeats Peres in Israeli elections.

1997 Hebron agreement signed by Netanyahu and Arafat

1998 Wye River Agreement between Israel and Palestinians

1999 Ehud Barak defeats Netanyahu in Israeli general election

2000 Final Israeli withdrawal from Lebanon.
Camp David talks fail to reach a final settlement.

2001 Sharon elected Israeli prime minister

2002 After continuing violence, Israel declares itself "at war" with Palestinians

Suggested Reading

Corzine, Phyllis. *The Palestinian-Israeli Accord (Lucent Overview Series).* San Diego, CA: Lucent Books Inc., 1997.

Gottfried, Ted. *The Israeli and Palestinians: Small Steps to Peace (Headliners).* Brookfield, CT: Millbrook Press Inc., 2000.

Harris, Nathaniel. *Israel and Arab Nations in Conflict (New Perspectives).* New York: Raintree Steck-Vaughn Publishers, 1999.

Marshood, Nabil. *Palestinian: Teenage Refugees and Immigrants Speak Out (In Their Own Voices).* New York: Rosen Publishing Group Inc., 1997.

McAleavy, Tony. *The Arab-Israeli Conflict (Cambridge History Program).* New York: SIGS Books & Multimedia, 1998.

Wagner, Heather Lehr. *Israel and the Arab World (People at Odds).* Broomall, PA: Chelsea House Publishers, 2002.

Glossary

anti-Semitism actions or feelings of hatred toward Jewish people

Arab a Semitic people (originally from Arabia) who live in an area stretching from North Africa to the Middle East

austere severe in attitude, especially regarding strict economic measures

British Mandate the period of British rule in Palestine after World War I. Britain ran Palestine on behalf of the League of Nations.

buffer zones territory seized by Israel in order to lessen the danger or reduce the impact of direct attack on Israel itself

ceasefire a temporary truce in which time a permanent peace may be negotiated

citizen a member of a society; **citizenship** brings rights and duties in a society

civilian a person who is not a member of the armed forces

coalition a temporary alliance, particularly of political parties in government

Cold War the state of hostility between Soviet powers and Western powers after World War II

Communism a political ideology that supports a classless society in which private ownership has been abolished

developed world the richer, industrial nations of the world

Diaspora the expulsion of the Jews from Palestine by the Romans in 100 A.D.

exile a long, usually enforced, absence from one's home or country

extradition handing over someone accused of a crime to the authorities of the country in which the crime was committed

Fedayeen an Arabic term meaning "self sacrificers," used by Palestinians who carried out raids against Israel in the early years of the conflict

fundamentalist someone who believes in strictly following religious rules, e.g., of the Bible or the Koran, the holy book of Islam

guerrilla a soldier who prefers tactics such as ambushes and hit-and-run raids over open battles, usually against a superior military force

Haganah a Jewish defense force set up in the 1920s

Holocaust the mass murder of Jews by the Nazis during World War II

Intifada a Palestinian uprising against Israeli rule in the Occupied Territories

Islam the religion based on the teachings of the prophet Mohammad, as laid down in the Koran

Jew one of the Hebrew people descended from the ancient Israelites

Judaism the religion of the Jews, based on the Old Testament and the Talmud

Knesset the parliament of modern Israel

League of Nations an international organization formed in 1919 to settle disputes between states without war; later replaced with the United Nations

militia a loose-knit, non-professional body of fighters

Muslim a follower of the Islamic faith

nationalism the belief that individual communities and cultures should act independently; to be nationalized implies pride in one's country and culture

nomadic continually moving from place to place, with no permanent home

Occupied Territories the areas captured by the Israelis during the 1967 Six-Day War: the West Bank, Gaza, and Jericho

Orthodox conforming to strict and established views and rules in a religion

Ottoman Empire the former Turkish Empire in Europe, Asia and Africa, which lasted from the 13th century until the end of World War I

Palestinian Liberation Organization (PLO) a political and military body set up in 1964 to defend the rights of Palestinian Arabs

Palestinian National Authority the name for the Palestinian government of the West Bank and Gaza territories after self-rule, 1994

Palestinians Arabs expelled from Palestine during the 1948 war

partition division into two or more parts

Passover Jewish festival commemorating the liberation of the Israelites from Egypt

pogrom the organized massacre of the Jews in Russia in the 1880s

reprisals action taken in retaliation against an enemy designed to discourage them from repeating an attack

sanctions the banning of trade in certain products, e.g., weapons, with a country in order to pressure it into changing policy

secular concerned with social and worldly matters rather than religious ones

superpower a country with immense economic and political influence and military (including nuclear) strength; usually refers to the United States and the Soviet Union

United Nations (UN) an international body set up in 1945 as a forum for settling disputes between nations

veto the right or power to reject something in a vote, overruling all other votes

Zionism a form of Jewish nationalism, originally dedicated to the creation of a Jewish state, now supportive of a strong Israel

Zionist a follower of the principles of Zionism

Index

Arafat, Yasir 13, 14–15, 36, 49, 50–51, 53, 54, 55, 57
Assad, Hafiz al 29, 31, 32

Balfour Declaration 16
Barak, Ehud 55, 57
Begin, Menachem 19, 32, 33, 34, 35, 45
Beirut 7, 37, 38, 39, 42, 46
Ben-Gurion, David 10, 18, 19, 22
Black September 13, 40–41

Camp David Agreement (1978) 32, 33, 34, 35, 53
Camp David talks (2000) 55, 56, 59

Egypt 5, 10, 21–23, 24, 26, 28, 29, 30, 31, 32, 33, 40, 45, 51

Fedayeen 20, 21, 23, 36

Gaza Strip 15, 27, 33, 48, 53, 55, 58
Golan Heights 25, 26, 27, 29, 32
Great Britain 12, 16, 17, 20, 21–22, 23, 30

Haganah 18, 19, 54
HAMAS 13, 14, 48, 53–54, 55, 57
Hebron and Wye River agreements (1997, 1998) 55
Hezbollah 13, 39
hijacks 40, 41, 46
Holocaust 9, 10, 11, 16, 17, 44
Hussein, King 36, 40
Hussein, Saddam 50
Intifada 47, 48–49, 50, 53

Iran 39, 42, 43
Iraq 18, 23, 50
Irgun 17, 19, 32, 35
"Iron-fist" policy 48, 51
Islam 4, 13, 59
Islamic fundamentalists 34, 42, 46, 48

Jerusalem 7, 11, 12, 17, 18, 26, 57, 59
Jordan 10, 36, 40, 51, 53

Knesset 10, 32, 34, 35, 39, 57

Lebanon 10, 14, 23, 35, 36–39, 40, 42, 45, 52
Libya 6, 42, 43, 47
Lockerbie 42, 43

Meir, Golda 28

Nasser, Gamal Abdel 21, 22, 23, 24, 25, 26, 28, 33
Netanyahu, Benjamin 53, 54, 55

Occupied Territories 14, 49, 50, 55, 57, 58
OPEC 30, 31
Oslo Accords (1993) 14, 15, 53, 54, 55, 58

Palestine Liberation Organization (PLO) 13, 14, 15, 24, 25, 27, 36, 37, 38, 39, 40, 43, 49, 50, 51, 52, 53, 54
Palestinian National Authority 15, 55
Palestinians 4, 10, 12–15, 17, 18, 19, 20, 27, 32, 40, 47, 48–49, 53, 55, 57, 58, 59
Peres, Shimon 15, 49, 55
Popular Front for the Liberation of Palestine (PFLP) 13, 40, 46

Rabin, Yitzhak 15, 32, 47, 49, 50, 53, 54
refugee camps 12, 13, 19, 20

Sadat, Anwar 28–29, 32, 33, 34, 35
Shamir, Yitzhak 49, 51
Sharon, Ariel 38, 46, 56, 57
Shiite Muslims 37, 38, 39, 42
Sinai 7, 22, 23, 26, 27, 28, 29, 32, 33, 34
Six-Day War (1967) 24–27, 35, 36, 45
Soviet Union 5, 6, 21, 23, 24, 28, 29, 30
Suez 4, 6, 20–23, 26, 29, 33, 45
Suez–Sinai War (1956) 20–23
Syria 5, 18, 24, 25, 29, 32, 34, 37, 39, 40, 42, 43

terrorism 6, 14, 38, 40–42, 43, 46, 47

United Arab Republic (UAR) 24
United Nations (UN) 6, 13, 17, 23, 25, 30, 37, 42
United States 5, 6, 7, 10, 20, 21, 23, 28, 29, 30, 32, 39, 42, 43, 47, 49, 50

War of Independence (1948) 13, 18, 19, 20
West Bank 15, 26, 27, 32, 33, 40, 47, 48, 49, 54, 55, 58, 59

Yom Kippur War (1973) 29, 30, 31, 32

Zionism 9, 10, 16, 17, 20, 50